Reflections on Issues in Music and Worship

by
Michael G. Coleman

TEACH Services, Inc.
P U B L I S H I N G
www.TEACHServices.com • (800) 367-1844

World rights reserved. This book or any portion thereof may not be copied or reproduced in any form or manner whatever, except as provided by law, without the written permission of the publisher, except by a reviewer who may quote brief passages in a review.

The author assumes full responsibility for the accuracy of all facts and quotations as cited in this book. The opinions expressed in this book are the author's personal views and interpretations, and do not necessarily reflect those of the publisher.

This book is provided with the understanding that the publisher is not engaged in giving spiritual, legal, medical, or other professional advice. If authoritative advice is needed, the reader should seek the counsel of a competent professional.

Copyright © 2019 Michael G. Coleman

Copyright © 2019 TEACH Services, Inc.

ISBN-13: 978-1-4796-1037-2 (Paperback)

ISBN-13: 978-1-4796-1038-9 (ePub)

Library of Congress Control Number: 2019933344

All scripture quotations, unless otherwise indicated, are taken from the New King James Version® unless otherwise stated. Copyright © 1982 by Thomas Nelson. Used by permission. All rights reserved.

Texts marked (KJV) are taken from the King James Version. Public Domain

Table of Contents

Introduction... 6

CHAPTER 1: The Thing I Did Not Know About Contemporary
Christian Music 8

CHAPTER 2: Leadership in Worship and Music: Biblical Examples and
Contemporary Challenges; Lessons from David and the Levites 18

CHAPTER 3: An Open Letter to Dr. Jesse Wilson, Chairman of the
Pastoral Evangelism Leadership Council, Oakwood University 32
      Part One 32
      Part Two 46

Summary 58

This book is dedicated to my three wonderful daughters:
Sarah, Moriah, and Nadine.

They have been blessed with inspiring and skillful musical abilities. As they use their gifts and talents to praise God and inspire humanity, I pray that this book would provide guidance to them and also to many other young people.

Introduction

Within the past four decades, the subjects of music and worship have sparked heated debates and controversies within the Seventh-day Adventist Church and the larger Christian community. These debates tend to revolve around whether or not certain kinds of Contemporary Christian Music (CCM) is appropriate for worship, whether Christian lyrics should be combined with popular dance tunes that have a pronounced and sustained rhythmic beat, and whether Adventists should adopt the styles and methods of the Charismatic/Pentecostal Movement. Questions such as "What's wrong with the use of drums in church?" and "Aren't hymns and anthems by-products of Eurocentrism?" have become staples in the ongoing debate.

As a pastor in the New York metropolitan area for the last twenty-nine years, I have been a participant in deliberations and conferences on music and worship. Two hitherto unpublished documents that I have written are particularly insightful in addressing contemporary issues in music and worship from different contexts. These two documents form the bulk of the contents of this book. However, they are presented in different sections of the book.

In an essay entitled, "The Thing I Did Not Know About Contemporary Christian Music," I present a reflection on the appropriateness of CCM

6   *Reflections on Issues in Music and Worship*

from historical, experiential, and biblical standpoints. This essay was distributed to delegates at a music workshop, at which I was a presenter, held by the Northeastern Conference in the spring of 2014. It provides both an experiential and a critical perspective of Contemporary Christian Music. Moreover, it delves into some sobering and challenging issues concerning CCM in a balanced manner. Specifically, the essay reveals that CCM has been influenced in an ironic way by the popular rock music that celebrated the sexually permissive and anti-Christian phase of the social revolution of the 1960s. However, the essay also shows that there are some good musical compositions that emanate from CCM. This essay comprises the first chapter of the book. It is rendered in the same form in which it was originally written, with only minor editing.

The second chapter of the book examines the importance of strong spiritual leadership in worship, music, and discipleship. Biblical examples and research from scholars and Christian leaders show that strong and stable spiritual leadership is necessary for churches to thrive. When such leadership is absent, problems take root and often manifest themselves in public worship and music.

The third chapter of the book features "An Open Letter" that I addressed to the chairman of the Pastoral Evangelism and Leadership Council (PELC) at Oakwood University concerning the emergence of the Charismatic/Pentecostal Movement at the PELC meetings and among Adventist pastors. The letter has a personal and historical feel to it for it is presented in this book with only minor editorial changes. Nevertheless, it addresses issues that are universal concerning Christianity and Adventism. This "Open Letter" was written as one continuous document in the winter of 2013. However, in this book, the Open Letter is divided into two parts. Part 1 begins by distinguishing some positive stylistic elements in traditional Black Preaching from the hazards of Charismatic/Pentecostal methods, however, it also shows that charismatic influences are now clearly present in Adventist churches of various races and ethnicities. Further, it shows from the Bible and the Spirit of Prophecy that the Charismatic/Glossolalia Movement is a by-product of a counterfeit revival that had its birth shortly after the Great Disappointment of 1844.

Part 2 of "An Open Letter" provides a discourse on what kinds of music is appropriate for Christians' enjoyment and worship. It highlights the point that not only the lyrics of a song communicates to us, the instrumental composition also communicates in a nonverbal manner. Thus, for example, when Christian lyrics are combined with rock or R&B genres, the mood created from the music will often be antithetical to the values expressed in the lyrics. This section of "An Open Letter" also makes a distinction between sacred music from African-American heritage and the worldly musical compositions of some African-American musicians that sought to blend the sacred with the profane.

Rather than a linear chapter-by-chapter discussion on music and worship, this book provides multiple reflections on these topics from different contexts. Readers are given a variety of frames from which they can glean insights on the subjects. The essay on CCM, the exposition on leadership in music and worship, and "An Open Letter" all address the topics from different angles.

CHAPTER 1

The Thing I Did Not Know About Contemporary Christian Music

As an unconverted non-church affiliated teenager in the second half of the 1970s, my life revolved around worldly entertainment, such as going to parties, drinking pink and golden champagne, periodically smoking marijuana, and even sneaking into a nightclub around my 15th birthday— two or three years under the club's legally permitted age. Much of what I enjoyed then involved popular music. I was fond of listening and dancing to disco, reggae, hip-hop, rap, and sometimes R&B, jazz, and calypso. I was not cognizant at that time that the above musical idioms were closely linked to the revolutionary rock of the 1960s, the rock 'n' roll of the 1950s, and the R&B, blues, jazz, and ragtime of the pre-World War II era. Nor was I aware that some historians, musicologists, theologians, behavioral scientists, educators, and medical doctors have drawn attention to the adverse impact of rock music on people.[1] Some of these experts have

---

1   See John Diamond, *Behavioral Kinesiology* (New York: Harper & Row, Publishers, 1979), pp. 93–106; Allan Bloom, *The Closing Of The American Mind* (New York: Simon and Schuster, 1987), pp. 68–81. Samuel Bacchiocchi, ed., *The Christian & Rock Music* (Berrien Springs, MI: Biblical Perspectives, 2000).

even highlighted the influential role of rock and its related hybrids in promoting a cultural revolution characterized by sexually promiscuity, drug abuse, hedonism, violence, irreverence, rebellion, occultism, relativism, and anti-Christian notions.[2]

However, the thing that I was most unconscious of at the time was that Contemporary Christian Music (CCM), the music that seemed to be in vogue among some youths and adults in the Seventh-day Adventist Church around the time of my conversion in the 1980s, had strong affinities to the rock music of the 1950s and 60s. I certainly did not know at the time that rock 'n' roll borrowed not only from the popular secular idioms that preceded it but also from African American gospel music and Charismatic/Pentecostal gospel songs.[3] Nor did I know that by the late 1960s, rock music influenced not only white gospel music, but also black gospel music, and virtually every form of CCM. Moreover, I had no idea at the time that CCM—the music that would eventually become the substitute for the secular music I once listened to—was following a similar trajectory of becoming increasingly more permissive, sensual, and loud as secular rock. I did not have a clue that many CCM musicians exhibit some of the same carnal behaviors as their secular counterparts.

Former CCM worship leader, Dan Lucarini, acknowledged that popular CCM artists imitate secular musicians in music performance, dress, and merchandising. According to Lucarini, these artists have become role models to young people in "indecent dress, rebellious images, improper crushes on married men by young girls," and "lustful interest in sexy females by adolescent males."[4]

Perhaps, in retrospect, I had witnessed a token of the unwieldy nature of CCM when I attended a concert in New York in the early 1980s and saw a very famous Gospel/CCM musician, caught up in a moment of effusive emotional exhibition, virtually "moonwalked" like Michael Jackson across the stage. Today, it is no surprise that Gospel/CCM artists such as Richard Smallwood would produce Christian music designed to elevate one's thoughts to God, as is the case of the song "Total Praise," but also compose a more funk-sounding playful song, curiously blended with gospel lyrics, such as "Mender." Likewise, "A Little More" is one of the most beautifully balanced musical compositions on CeCe Winans's 2007

---

2   See Robert Pielke, *You Say You Want a Revolution* (Chicago: Nelson-Hall Publishers, 1986); Samuel Bacchiocchi, ed., *The Christian & Rock Music*.

3   See Martha Bayles, *Hole in Our Soul: the Lost of Beauty and Meaning in American Popular Music* (New York, Toronto, Oxford: The Free Press, 1994), pp. 127–200.

4   Dan Lucarini, *Why I Left the Contemporary Christian Music Movement* (New York: Evangelical Press, 2002), p. 117.

Pure Worship album (although the lyrical content is more appropriate for a love song); however, in another song entitled "All About You" on the same album, she dabbles in a mixture of worldly calypso and Christian lyrics. This is just the nature of the highly commercialized industry of CCM. In CCM, with very few exceptions, we are almost guaranteed that the same musician will produce both a sacred sounding composition and a questionable blend of the sacred and the profane. In spite of such disturbing mixtures, I am not advocating that Christians should avoid listening to CCM but rather that we should be highly selective in our listening and use of CCM, especially in worship.

> *I am not advocating that Christians should avoid listening to CCM but rather that we should be highly selective in our listening and use of CCM, especially in worship.*

If I had been quasi-ignorant in the early 1980s of Contemporary Christian Music's intimate relationship to popular secular music, by the mid-1990s, Rick Warren, one of the most popular pastors in the United States, was certainly not. In his book, *The Purpose Driven Church*, Warren stated the following:

> For the first time in history, there exists a universal music style that can be heard in every country of the world. It's called contemporary pop/rock. The same songs are being played on radios in Nairobi and Tokyo and Moscow. Most TV commercials use the contemporary/rock style. Even country and western has adapted it. This is the primary music style we've chosen to use at Saddleback.[5]

Warren further explained that the decision to promote CCM in his church's worship service came after he took a survey of his congregation at the Saddleback Valley Community Church in California and discovered that 96 percent of his members listened to contemporary pop/rock music on a regular basis. According to Warren, his members "like bright, happy, cheerful music with a strong beat. Their ears are accustomed to music with a strong bass line and rhythm."[6]

---

5 Rick Warren, *The Purpose Driven Church* (Grand Rapids, MI: Zondervan Pub. 1995), p. 285.
6 Ibid.

The Thing I Did Not Know About Contemporary Christian Music 11

It is unfortunate that Pastor Warren's primary criterion for the selection of music in his church service was a survey of what style of music his members enjoyed rather than a survey of what the Bible teaches concerning music. However, Warren is at least transparent about his actions. He is certainly correct in stating that the contemporary pop/rock style has become universal. And here lies one of the most disturbing reality that the Christian Church—both Protestant and Catholic—must deal with: namely, that the widespread acceptance of Contemporary Christian Music in our churches implies that contemporary pop/rock is as potent and universal in the church as it is in the world. The same musical style that has blatantly promoted antisocial behaviors, occultism, and de-Christianization has become the most celebrated music both in the world and in the church.

In medieval Europe, the music of the church influenced secular society so much so that secular folk tunes had a similar musical structure to religious music. It was therefore not difficult later on for the Protestant reformer, Martin Luther, to modify some of these folk songs into choral music for worship by employing the user-friendly melodic structure of the folk songs to replace the high-flown esoteric chants of much of the Roman Catholic influenced church music; this process is known as *contrafacta*. Thus, in spite of some of the negative hegemonic impact of Roman Catholicism in Western Europe during this era, Luther could still find elements in the secular music of his day that reflected the values of a Christian society. But today it is the musical style and structure of the world that is dominating the church.

There is a world of difference between Luther's day and our day. In Luther's day Christianity dominated society, in our day Christianity is sequestered to purely religious contexts. In Luther's day a medieval church-oriented musical structure was still predominant even in secular compositions, but in our day, it is a popular worldly-oriented musical structure that is dominating the music of the church. CCM, therefore, reflects a total reversal of what took place in Luther's time.

Perhaps, what might be helpful at this juncture is a brief history of how an alliance between Christianity and popular music gave birth to Contemporary Christian Music. In his book, *The Death of Christian Britain*, social and cultural historian, Callum Brown, provides a snippet view of the early 1960s in Britain when the Church of England and other Christian denominations sought to deal with the impact of rock music on its youth. According to Brown, many of these churches attempted "to compromise with the new age of youth in the late 1960s, developing new forms of religious worship using guitars and penny whistles, modern dress and a 'happy-clappy' atmosphere," all with the goal of capturing and retaining the youths that the *Beatles* and other rock artists seem to be leading astray. Brown reveals that he was among the teenagers that attended the many church-sponsored rock and disco dances but "the increasing loudness of the music, the arrival of soft drugs, the visits of the police, and, above all, the brazen nature of teenagers' casual sexual liaisons" led the church to abandon these strategies by the end of the decade.[7]

The churches in Britain were not successful in their quest to co-opt and sanitize rock music. Consequently, they were not able to stop the flow of young people away from Christian values. Today, Britain is no longer the largely Christian society that it once was before the 1960s. One of the most powerful factors in this dramatic decline of Christianity in Britain—which began in the 1960s and continues to the present—is, in my opinion, rock music in all its forms.

---

7   Callum Brown, *The Death of Christian Britain: Understanding Secularization, 1800–2000* (London and New York: Routledge, 2001), p. 180.

The Thing I Did Not Know About Contemporary Christian Music

Ironically, in the United States an interesting combination of conservative Evangelicals, the Jesus Movement, the music industry, and the film industry had more success than the churches in Britain in co-opting rock music for Christianity and marketing the contemporary Christian version of rock to a society that by the 1970s had become weary of the excesses of the 1960s rock culture. Depending on how one looks at it, this alliance between Evangelical Christianity and popular music was a clever strategy because the young people of the 1950s and 1960s who had been enamored with rock but had become disenchanted by its drug-oriented and antisocial culture could now keep their music, theoretically avoid its negative culture, and be a Christian all at the same time! And, what a windfall this was for the music and film industries! The music industry would market a newer and safer form of rock/pop, now with inspiring Christian lyrics, and the film industry would make millions of dollars on contemporary rock-based 'Jesus shows' such as *Jesus Christ Superstar* and *Godspell*.[8]

Yet from the very inception of what appeared to be a successful alliance between the church and the world in the American Contemporary Christian Music industry, the world held the trump card: much money could be made, and celebrities would be born. David Stowe, in his book, *No Sympathy for the Devil,* shares a very revealing vignette of how the producers of *Jesus Christ Superstar* were initially attempting to get the Beatles' superstar, the late John Lennon, to play the role of Jesus in the film. They even contemplated getting Lennon's wife, Yoko Ono, to play Mary Magdalene. While this part of the producers' plans did not materialize, *Jesus Christ Superstar* turned out to be a lucratively successful coalition between Christianity, pop/rock, and the film industry.[9]

However, it is shocking to know that this marriage between contemporary Christianity and pop/rock had initially contemplated using John Lennon—someone who had openly spoken disparagingly of Christianity—to play the role of Jesus in a film. In March 1966, John Lennon had told journalist Maureen Cleave of the London *Evening Standard* newspaper, "Christianity will go. It will vanish and shrink. I needn't argue about that, I'm right and will be proved right. We're more popular than Jesus right now."[10]

It is beyond the scope of this article to delve into other interesting aspects of the early alliance between pop/rock and Christianity in the

---

8   For a solid account of the history of CCM in America see David Stowe, *No Sympathy for the Devil* (Chapel Hill: University of North Carolina Press, 2011).
9   David Stowe, p. 43.
10 "How Does a Beatle Live? John Lennon Lives Like this", interview with John Lennon, *Evening Standard,* March 1966.

1970s and 1980s, such as CCM's ambivalent relationship with pop/rock celebrities like Little Richard, Aretha Franklin, Marvin Gaye, Al Green, Stevie Wonder, Johnny Cash, Bob Dylan and the group, Earth, Wind & Fire. Suffice it to say that while some early CCM musicians such as Andraé Crouch remained more or less within the orbit of the church, many others wallowed in the world while intermittently claiming to be followers of Christ.

Even today, we cannot ignore the reality that many CCM artists, including Mary Mary, Krystal Meyers, Kirk Franklin, Amy Grant, Fred Hammond, Hezekiah Walker, Yolanda Adams, and Pastor Donnie McClurkin have become increasingly comfortable with mimicking popular secular musicians and appealing to the tastes of worldly consumers. Today's CCM includes such dubious styles as Christian Heavy Metal and Christian Rap music.

My disenchantment with CCM is not due to a love for the classics and a dislike for anything contemporary or popular. Neither is it due to Eurocentric tastes and biases. To the contrary, much of my music orientation from the time I was converted in the early 1980s has been in the African American Gospel tradition. Moreover, I am attracted to several renditions in Contemporary Worship Music (CWM) that skillfully blend percussion with strings and wind instruments. I also appreciate the clear, straightforward, and soulful lyrics of some CCM songs. Hence, my concern is not with joyful and lively expressions of praise to God in CCM. I whole heartily embrace and promote a soulful worship experience.

Nevertheless, what I see as the major problems of CCM are its strong accented and incessant beats, its overall adoption of the essential structure of popular dance music (especially rock and R&B), and its subtle, ironic tendency to undermine Christian values. While rock music has and will continue to evolve, one of its more permanent features is its pronounced rhythmic structure and the overshadowing of melody and harmony by a persistent beat. For example, in 4/4 time, rock tends to emphasize the second and fourth beats; in 2/4 time, it accentuates the upbeat or backbeat. Yet rock's accentuation of these beats is not a momentary highlight in a musical composition, it is constant and often pronounced; sometimes it is soft and subtle but nevertheless constant, as is frequently the case in popular love songs. CCM has adopted the key rhythmic style of pop/rock music. Therefore, even though the lyrics of CCM is different, the musical structure is essentially the same as rock and the impact of this musical structure is consistent in arousing sensual feelings and stimulating people toward erotic bodily movements.

Although rock's musical structure is eclectic in that it draws on elements from blues, rhythm and blues, country and western, jazz, black gospel, and Charismatic/Pentecostal music, it nevertheless has as its common denominator a tendency to undermine moral values and the institutions that nurture these values: namely, the church and the family. Illicit sexuality and loose morals are virtually indigenous to rock music, and it, therefore, should be no surprise that this pattern is becoming more common in CCM because CCM is in essence pop/rock with Christian lyrics.

Rock music and other related dance music reflect (in both instrumentation and lyrics) principles and values that are incongruent with the gospel as outlined in Jesus' Sermon on the Mount in Matthew chapters 5–7. For example, Jesus promoted values of self-denial, righteousness, mercy, forgiveness, humility, meekness, honesty, integrity, and love; however, rock music regularly promotes lust, pride, jealousy, covetousness, vengeance, irreverence, sensuality, cupidity, relativism, hedonism, and materialism. Since CCM has adopted the musical structure of rock, it has also inadvertently imbibed some of the values of rock. If we were to take away the lyrics from many CCM compositions the thing that would be left is the musical structure and values of pop/rock.

Why would Christians use the same musical structure and genres that the world has used to promote sexual promiscuity, irreverence, and pride as music to glorify God? The Bible is clear in 1 John 2:15–16 that we should avoid those things that emphasize lust and pride:

> Do not love the world or the things in the world. If anyone loves the world, the love of the Father is not in him. For all that is in the world—the lust of the flesh, the lust of the eyes, and the pride of life—is not of the Father but is of the world. (NKJV)

Many of the musical compositions of CCM unwittingly promote pride and carnality in the instrumental composition even while the lyrics explicitly point to praising God. CCM did not come into being as a result of following the paradigm of music ministry that King David instituted when he commissioned the Levites to consecrate themselves to the task of rendering sacred music in the temple (1 Chronicles 16:1–7, 25:1–7). Nor did it originate as a result of imitating the *contrafacta* model established by Martin Luther: that of judiciously modifying folk music for sacred purposes. Rather, CCM came into being as a result of the church's conformity to the style and influence of popular, commercial secular music. It is frankly the values of the profit-driven pop/rock music industry that has been the most dominant influence in CCM, and this is really a microcosm of a broader conformity of contemporary Christianity to popular culture. In essence, worldly forces are impacting our manner of praise and worship.

> *CCM came into being as a result of the church's conformity to the style and influence of popular, commercial secular music.*

Again, even though the lyrics of CCM are often inspiring, its instrumental composition sends another message that is frequently totally contradictory to its lyrics. This becomes particularly problematic in the church worship service because the pronounced over-accentuated rhythmic structure of CCM is very conducive to the kind of dancing that is done in nightclubs, including the slow sensual type.

Lilianne Doukhan, professor of music at Andrews University and the Seventh-day Adventist Theological Seminary, highlighted the fact that "pronounced and sustained rhythm" can lead to a person becoming so absorbed in the enjoyment of the music that "there is a progressive loss of interest in the rational or cognitive control of the situation." Earlier in the same paragraph, she noted that the more we listen to pronounced rhythmic music the more our appetite grows for "stronger and more accented rhythms."[11] Although Doukhan seems to endorse CCM, she nevertheless underscored the bewitching power of pronounced and sustained rhythms.

With Doukhan's research in mind, I have observed over the past four decades that both pastors and church members have become increasingly more accepting of hard rock genres of music such as hip-hop, calypso, reggae, and heavy metal in the church, as long as these are blended with Christian lyrics. Thus, their appetites for heavier rhythms have indeed increased. I have also noticed that after a congregation has listened to fifteen to thirty minutes of CCM during the average praise and worship period, many in the congregation tend to respond to the preaching of the Word by rote rather than by critical thinking.

There are many African American Christians today who believe that the pronounced rhythmic music that is found in many popular secular songs and numerous CCM songs is a legitimate component of the spiritual heritage of Blacks. However, Eurydice Osterman, an African-American musicologist and former professor at Oakwood University, reminds us that pop/rock was not derived from African-American heritage music, such as

---

11 Lilianne Doukhan, *In Tune with God* (Hagerstown, MD: Autumn House, 2010), p. 30.

The Thing I Did Not Know About Contemporary Christian Music

Negro Spirituals, but from "secular and often irreligious music known as 'Rhythm and Blues.' This music became the expression of those Blacks who strayed from or rejected the Christian faith."[12] She also reminds us that Black heritage music is mainly melodic. These distinctions are very important as we examine CCM, which encompasses Black Gospel as well as other forms of popular Christian music.

I believe that CCM has gradually drifted toward the sensual and permissive. I also believe that CCM's drift toward worldliness was inevitable due to its dominant rock-based musical structure and its eclectic and relativistic attitude. CCM has thus become the proverbial frog in the kettle of rock rhythms and values. CCM has produced some inspiring sacred music. But unfortunately, like the Hollywood film industry, the bad of CCM far outweighs the good.

In conclusion, the thing I did not know about CCM at the time of my conversion to Christianity in the early 1980s is its strong association with pop/rock music. However, as I have examined CCM through historical, cultural, theological, and experiential lenses, I have come to believe that the wide acceptance of CCM in our churches today is evidence of contemporary Christianity's conformity to the world. I am nevertheless optimistic that this situation can be reversed. The good news is that the world's domination of the church in the form of contemporary Christian rock is still a relatively new phenomenon. It only began around the early 1970s. As of now, it has a much shorter lifespan than other issues to which large segments of the Christian church have in the past conformed to the world, such as in the case of slavery and racial discrimination. Though the process may be difficult, I am hopeful that by God's grace Christianity's enchantment with pop/rock will be reversed. I am also praying that there will be an explosion of the kind of Christian music that reflects, in both its instrumental and lyrical compositions, solid Biblical principles.

As mentioned, I am not proposing that we shun all Contemporary Christian Music, but rather, that we are judicious and highly selective of what we listen to and especially what we use in worship. I, therefore, pray that there will be a great movement in CCM away from the pop/rock idiom and toward more balanced contemporary compositions.

---

12 Eurydice Osterman, in Bacchiochi, ed, *The Christian & Rock Music* (Berrien Springs, MI: Biblical Perspectives), p. 302.

CHAPTER 2

Leadership in Worship and Music:
Biblical Examples and Contemporary Challenges
Lessons from David and the Levites

The Bible reveals a clear picture of God's expectations for His people in conducting worship and music. In 1 Chronicles chapters 15, 16, and 25 the Bible shows that King David, who himself was a skillful musician, chose certain priests or Levites to be in charge of worship and music. Let us notice some of the passages in the aforementioned chapters of 1 Chronicles that show how intentional David was in making sure that consecrated and skillful people were in charge of the music that was to be used in the worship of God:

> Then David spoke to the leaders of the Levites to appoint their brethren to be the singers accompanied by instruments of music, stringed instruments, harps, and cymbals, by raising the voice with resounding joy. So the Levites appointed Heman the son of Joel; and of his brethren, Asaph the son of Berechiah; and of their brethren, the sons of Merari, Ethan the son of Kushaiah. (1 Chron. 15:16–17, NKJV)

Leadership in Worship and Music:

> Moreover David and the captains of the army separated for the service some of the sons of Asaph, of Heman, and of Jeduthun, who should prophesy with harps, stringed instruments, and cymbals. (1 Chron. 25:1 NKJV)

David was consistent in his selection of sanctified and skillful leaders in both the worship that occasioned the transportation of the ark of the covenant and the regular worship for the temple services in Jerusalem. The appointment of leaders from among the priesthood to be the musicians for worship was a clear indication by David that the music designed for the worship of God was to be of a sacred and special nature. Only a holy order of leaders was to focus their attention on designing music for the praise of God and the spiritual elevation of Israel. Consecration was one of the two major criteria that David used to decide who should be put in charge of music and worship. The other criterion was musical skill. 1 Chronicles 15:22 makes this very clear: "Chenaniah, leader of the Levites, was instructor in charge of the music, because he was skillful."

Today many Adventists churches lack consecrated and skillful musicians because they have not made these criteria a priority in their selection of church musicians. Sometimes musicians are chosen who are clearly skillful but lack consecration, and at other times consecrated people are selected to function as church musicians, but they are diminished in skill. Both consecration and musical skill are indispensable for the production of sacred music.

The fact that the musicians that David chose were all members of the priesthood indicates that they were supported by the tithes to do their sacred work. With income from the tithes, these musicians could focus their attention on their mission and ministry without worrying about doing other jobs to earn wages. Furthermore, since the task of composing and performing sacred music was entrusted to specific leaders of families among the Levites, it meant that these leaders would mentor and train their descendants to continue the legacy of exhibiting the best in music and worship. David's plan, therefore, ensured that there would be on-going education and mentorship in music and worship and that there would be no dearth of consecrated and skillful musicians for the service of God.

One of the most conspicuous problems in the areas of worship and music in the Seventh-day Adventist Church today is the lack of a strategy for the training, mentorship, employment, and continuity of Adventist musicians for our worship services. Consequently, some of our churches are obliged to employ musicians who are not Seventh-day Adventists in order fill the void of not being able to find an Adventist musician. Furthermore, due to lack of financial support from their local congregation, some Adventists musicians seek employment in other denominations; thus they focus their energies on rendering music for worship services on Sundays.

The worst impact of the church's lack of intentionality in providing for the education, mentorship, and succession of Adventist musicians is the resultant lack of commitment to the core values of the church by some of our own musicians. The Seventh-day Adventist denomination has some of the most dedicated and skillful musicians in the world. However, in some cases, Adventist musicians perform songs and compositions in worship services that gradually undermine our fundamental beliefs. For example, some Adventists musicians have introduced songs at funeral services and at Sabbath worship services that celebrate going to heaven at death. Others have combined Christian lyrics with popular genres such as rock, hip-hop, R&B, reggae, and calypso; and they introduced these worldly compositions in Adventist worship services or sometimes in children's songs for Vacation Bible School.

David's Model Applied to Conferences and Churches

The paradigm of leadership in worship and music that David established for Israel has some worthwhile applications to the leadership of conference administrators, pastors, and elders. David role as king over Israel was that of the chief administrator over the chosen people. When David entrusted the music into the hands of the priests who were ordained by God to lead out in worship, he made a wise decision because music is an integral part of worship and the leaders who are in charge of designing and executing worship should be the ones that oversee music.

Executive leaders of state and regional conferences are the chief administrators of the churches within their territories. Have conference administrators followed David's example in placing music in the hands of the pastors—the contemporary leaders who have been set apart to be the main overseers of worship in the churches? I do not mean to imply that pastors should be praise team leaders, choir directors, or plan the details of music instead of a music coordinator. However, I wish to convey that pastors should be in charge of making sure that there is education, mentorship, and best practices in music and worship in the congregations which they lead. Furthermore, pastors should be directly involved in the selection of musicians for their congregations. They also should develop a strategy for the continuity of musicians. In some conferences the executive administrators have clearly stated that pastors should be the main overseers of both worship and music in their churches. However, in other conferences, this matter is not clear, and consequently, their pastors tend to focus on preaching, visitation, and chairing the church board, but they leave worship and music exclusively under the governance of others.

Music is an integral part of worship and the leaders who are in charge of designing and executing worship should be the ones that oversee music.

Yet, even in conferences where music and worship have been entrusted to the pastorate, there are still some problems. One problem is that many pastors feel ill-equipped to lead out in worship beyond preaching and praying, not to mention the responsibility of overseeing music. This problem can be solved at the seminary and conference levels, as both entities should provide a strategy, in consultation with each other, for the education of pastors in leading music and worship in the church. In this regard, mentorship from consecrated, experienced, and skillful pastors should be a core component of such education.

Another problem is that some pastors adopt an eclectic approach to music and worship, which means that they direct their musicians to use whatever genres and blends of music that will attract people to their worship services, with little regard to biblical principles and guidance from the writings of Ellen White. When these pastors are questioned as to why they allow almost any kind of music in the church, some of them retort by saying that the Seventh-day Adventist Church does not have a theology of music, therefore, they are free to use whatever music will motivate people to attend church. Others claim that the tide towards blending popular secular genres with Christian lyrics has become so strong and entrenched in the church that to resist it would only lead to controversy: they would be stigmatized as ultra conservatives and traditionalists.

In light of these problems, there is a grave and urgent need for conference administrators to bring their pastors together in Bible conferences and workers' meetings to carefully study and deliberate on the subjects of music and worship, and to also receive training in these areas. Conference administrators should also include elders in these deliberations and training because elders can also be viewed as contemporary counterparts to the Levites in that elders are local overseers of the church. Moreover, conference administrators would do well if they could work out a strategy for the employment of consecrated musicians in the churches.

The Perspective of the New Testament

The New Testament has a few passages that address the topic of leadership in worship and music. For example, 1 Corinthians 14 deals with the issue of speaking in tongues in public worship. Evidently, although the church at Corinth was endowed with the gift of speaking in different languages in combination with other spiritual gifts, some members of the church were abusing the gift of tongues by pridefully showcasing their ability without seeking to enrich the understanding of other members. This is why Paul states the following in 1 Corinthians 14:4–12:

> He who speaks in a tongue edifies himself, but he who prophesies edifies the church. I wish you all spoke with tongues but even more that you prophesied; for he who prophesies is greater than he who speaks with tongues, unless indeed he interprets, that the church may receive edification. But now, brethren, if I come to you speaking with tongues, what shall I profit you unless I speak to you either by revelation, by knowledge, by prophesying, or by teaching? Even things without life, whether flute or harp, when they make a sound, unless they make a distinction in the sounds, how will it be known what is piped or played? For if the trumpet makes an uncertain sound, who will prepare for battle? So likewise you, unless you utter by the tongue words easy to understand, how will it be known what is spoken? For you will be speaking into the air.

There are, it may be, so many kinds of languages in the world, and none of them is without significance. Therefore, if I do not know the meaning of the language, I shall be a foreigner to him who speaks, and he who speaks will be a foreigner to me. Even so you, since you are zealous for spiritual gifts, let it be for the edification of the church that you seek to excel. (1 Cor. 14:4–12, NKJV)

Notice again that Paul's main point in the above passage is that the gift of tongues should be used only in a manner in which it edifies the church at large and not merely the individual who has the gift. In order to accomplish this, Paul instructs the church at Corinth that whenever people speak in tongues in public worship, the leaders of worship should always provide for the interpretation of the foreign language so that the entire church may benefit. Paul repeatedly emphasizes this point in more than one place in 1 Corinthians 14 (e.g., verses 5, 27, 28); however, it comes across forcefully in verse 28: "But if there is no interpreter, let him keep silent in church, and let him speak to himself and to God."

The abuse of the gift of tongues was one of several problems among the Corinthian Christians. Paul heard that among these believers were self-serving displays of spiritual gifts, attention-seeking exhibitions in public worship, and divisions into cliques. He highlights in verse 26 the confusion caused by these problems when the church members came together: "How is it then, brethren? Whenever you come together, each of you has a psalm, has a teaching, has a tongue, has a revelation, has an interpretation." Paul admonishes the church to "Let all things be done for edification" (vs. 26), and "Let all things be done decently and in order" (vs. 40).

Seventh-day Adventist congregations are not immune to the problems that were present in the church at Corinth. In some of our churches, it can be seen that there is an absence of coordination and collaboration in worship and music. For example, in some of our churches, the organist plays in a manner that overpowers the accompanying pianist, while the drummer overshadows all sounds with a constant, uninterrupted loud-sounding beat. Furthermore, in some churches, one is likely to hear the sounds of various instruments—such as bass guitars, saxophones, and tambourines—all competing for attention rather than rendering a harmonious musical presentation. The problem is not the number and diversity of instruments but the lack of coordination and harmony among the musicians. While there should be hearty expressions of praise to God in worship, in some churches, there is often too much independent exhibition, prideful attention-seeking, and over-zealous outbursts at the expense of disturbing the peace of other members of the congregation. Paul's admonition to "let all things be done for edification" and "let all things be done decently and in order" is certainly relevant to these kinds of problem in worship services.

I would like to suggest that there was another problem among the Corinthian believers that is not explicitly cited by Paul in the two epistles to the Corinthians that we have in the Bible. However, the problem is implied by such things as the multiplicity of conflicts and personal agendas among the believers, the presence of several factions within the church that claim that they are the direct and exclusive followers of either Paul or Apollos or Peter or Christ, the lack of decisive and redemptive disciplinary action for members in engaged in repulsive immoral conduct, and the habit of settling disputes among believers in court (1 Cor. 1:12; 3:3–4; 1 Cor. 5; 1 Cor. 6:1). The specific problem of which I speak is the absence of stable spiritual leadership among the Christians of Corinth at the time that Paul wrote his epistles to the church. To be clear, the need for sustainable spiritual leadership was not the root of all the problems that the Corinthian believers were facing. However, most of the problems

Leadership in Worship and Music: 25

flourished like weeds in an unmanaged garden due to instability in spiritual leadership.

What do we know about the history of leadership in the Corinthian church? We know from Acts 18 that Paul, accompanied by Silas, Timothy, and Aquila and Priscilla, labored in Corinth for a year and a half and planted a thriving church with many new converts (Acts 18:8–11). The city of Corinth, located in Greece, was a major commercial center in the Roman Empire. It was known for luxury, idolatry, and licentiousness. Some of the new converts were people who had once engaged in extortion, drunkenness, idolatry, adultery, and homosexuality but now they were justified and sanctified by the Lord Jesus and the Holy Spirit (1 Cor. 6:9–11). Notwithstanding the effective leadership of Paul in planting the church and nurturing its new members for eighteen months, there is little evidence of stability in the spiritual leadership of the church after Paul and his team left.

According to Acts 19:1, after Paul left Corinth to minister at Ephesus, Apollos came there and further enlarged and nurtured the church. However, during the time that Apollos was providing leadership to the believers at Corinth, partisanship, competitiveness, and conflicts arose among these members. Specifically, some of the members began to compare Paul's fairly new approach of preaching the simple gospel of Christ to the Gentiles (without presenting sophisticated arguments of logic that the Greeks loved to hear) with Apollos's sophisticated arguments. They also noticed that in a short time Apollos's ministry (building on the foundation laid by Paul) resulted in many new converts. Consequently, some of the church members concluded that Apollos is a greater minister than Paul and they began to pridefully claim that they were disciples of Apollos. However, according to Ellen G. White, "Paul and Apollos were in perfect harmony."[13] Neither Apollos or Paul allowed the factions in the church to stir competition and pride between them. Yet, in order not to be associated with the group of members that was exalting him and instigating conflict in the church Apollos departed rather suddenly from Corinth. Although Paul urged him to return to Corinth and continue his work, Apollos was so hurt by the partisanship in the church that he declined to return during those difficult times.[14]

We can only imagine that with the vacuum in solid spiritual leadership caused by the departure of Apollos, problems proliferated and intensified in the Corinthian church. Because of his active evangelistic labors at

---

13 Ellen G. White, *Acts of the Apostles* (Nampa, ID, Pacific Press Publishing Association), p. 280.
14 Ibid., p. 280.

Ephesus, Paul was obliged to provide counsel to the church at Corinth from long distance via his epistles to the Corinthians, and therefore, it took a long time before healing, spiritual growth, and strong spiritual leadership remerged in the church.

Again, the problems that arose in public worship in 1 Corinthians 14 reflect the reality of a larger problem: the instability in spiritual leadership. The point I am making is that strong godly leadership is an effective remedy for most of the problems that the church faces in regard to public worship. When this kind of leadership is absent, problems will often manifest themselves in public worship and music; furthermore, these problems will likely take root and thrive. It is therefore incumbent on pastors and elders to provide strong and stable spiritual leadership to their congregations.

> *Strong godly leadership is an effective remedy for most of the problems that the church faces in regard to public worship.*

Another New Testament passage of Scripture that shows the importance of leadership in worship is found in the fourth and fifth chapters of Revelation. Notwithstanding the symbolic nature of Revelation, in chapters 4 and 5 we can clearly see a glorious and sublime scene of worship to God. What is very significant for our purpose is the leadership of twenty-four elders in this awesome heavenly worship scene. They prostrate themselves before the throne of God, offer prayers, shout praise, play their harps, and sing a new song to the Lord (Rev. 5:8–14). Who are these twenty-four elders? What is the significance of their participation and leadership in this heavenly worship scene?

Bible scholars have not reached a consensus on who the twenty-four elders are. Adventists tend to believe that the twenty-four elders are literal people in heaven and that they were among the saints that were resurrected at the time of Jesus's resurrection; they being the first-fruits of the resurrection to come at Christ's second coming (Matt. 27:52–53). Others view the twenty-four elders as symbolizing the totality of God's people in that the twenty-four elders are made up of the twelve patriarchs of the tribes of Israel and the twelve apostles. Some scholars believe that the twenty-four elders represent the twenty-four courses of the Levitical priesthood. Others believe that the twenty-four elders represent unfallen beings.[15]

---

15 Francis D. Nichol, Ed., *Seventh-day Adventist Bible Commentary*, vol. 7 (Washington, D.C.: Review and Herald Publishing Association, 1980), pp. 767–8.

Notwithstanding the variation in interpretation, none of the above interpretations is opposed to the notion that the twenty-four elders signify spiritual leadership. Whether the twenty-four elders are human or unfallen beings, whether they are literal or symbolic, their roles involve spiritual leadership. In both the Old and New Testaments, the role of elders entailed spiritual leadership. The fact that the twenty-four elders are depicted in the fourth and fifth chapters of Revelation as leading out in worship with songs of praise and harps before the throne of God should inspire pastors and elders—the primary spiritual leaders of the church—to take their rightful place as leaders in worship and music.

Contemporary Leadership Challenges

The need for strong spiritual leadership has been gaining more ground in the past three decades as scholars and Christian leaders have taken notice of contemporary Christianity's lack of focus on the Great Gospel Commission and its weakness in the area of discipleship.[16] For example, Bill Hybels, the widely esteemed pastor of the Willow Creek Community Church in Chicago (a non-denominational church), acknowledged in 2007, to the dismay of many pastors, that though his "seeker sensitive" approach to church growth has increased his membership and brought enthusiasm to his church, it has failed to produce members who are spiritually mature.[17]

The seeker sensitive model involved a deemphasis of traditional methods of evangelism and discipleship such as doctrinal preaching, calling for repentance from sin, and committing one's self to giving Bible studies; rather, it focused on innovation and meeting the wants of people—often dubbed "felt needs"—in a similar manner to how businesses seek to know the desires of customers and consumers and then develop a marketing plan to address them. The seeker sensitive paradigm created an atmosphere where many people were present for worship services, but they were not growing spiritually. This atmosphere allowed members to think that "jazzing up" the worship service with CCM was a necessary innovation for the church to grow. The seeker sensitive model also caused

---

16 See Eric Geiger, Michael Kelly, and Philip Nation, *Transformational discipleship: How people really grow* (Nashville, TN: B&H Books, 2012); Christian Schwartz, *Natural church development: A guide to eight essential qualities of healthy churches* (Carol Stream, IL: ChurchSmart Resources, 1996); Dallas Willard, *The great omission: Reclaiming Jesus's essential teachings on discipleship* (San Francisco, CA: HarperOne, 2006).

17 See Bob Burney, "A shocking 'confession' from Willow Greek Community Church," *Town Hall*, (2007, October 30). Retrieved from http://1ref.us/ra, accessed December 19, 2018. Also, Gary L. Hawkins and Cally Parkinson, *Reveal: Where are You?* (Chicago, Il: Willow Creek Association, 2007).

people to view Christianity as something "cool" and made them feel comfortable in "dressing down" to attend church worship service, sometimes in jeans and a t-shirt. However, it resulted in producing spiritually weak Christians who were pastor-dependent and not committed to making disciples for Christ.

The rethinking that has been taking place among Christian leaders concerning discipleship and spiritual leadership has yielded some interesting insights. For example, Alan Hirsch has highlighted the vicious cycle that many pastors and churches get into in their attempts to attract people to the church services by implementing the latest church growth program rather than by going out of the church building to make disciples for Christ. *The attractional model* is the name given by Hirsch and others to the common approach of attracting people to the church worship services rather than going out of the church edifice to reach people where they are.[18] Hirsch observed that the attractional model is not making an impact on the decline of Christianity in the world or on the spiritual growth of church members. In the following statement he emphasized that many church leaders continue to follow the same attractional approach in spite of the fact that Christianity is on a decline in the world:

> What is becoming increasingly clear is that if we are going to meaningfully reach the majority of people, we are not going to be able to do it by simply doing more of the same. And yet it seems that when faced with our problems of decline, we automatically reach for the latest church growth package to solve the problem—we seem to have nowhere else to go. But simply pumping up the programs, improving the music and audiovisual effects, or jiggering the ministry mix won't solve our missional crisis. Something far more fundamental is needed.[19]

Hirsch's reference to "pumping up the programs, improving the music and audiovisual effects" in order to draw crowds of people to the church worship services is certainly what many churches are doing today yet they are not experiencing healthy numerical and spiritual growth. According to Hirsch, much of the growth that Christianity has experienced in the past few decades have not come from conversion but from members that switched from one church to another. In the following statement he makes his case:

---

18 Alan Hirsch, *The Forgotten Ways* (Grand Rapids, MI: Brazos Press, 2006); Randy Pope, *Insourcing: Bringing discipleship back to the local church* (Grand Rapids, MI: Zondervan, 2013).
19 Hirsch, p. 37.

Statistics right across the Western world where this model hold sway indicate that the vast majority of the church's growth comes from 'switchers'—people who move from one church to another based on the perception and experience of the programming. There is precious little conversion growth. No one really gets to see the problem, because it 'feels so right' and it 'works for me.' In fact, the church is on the decline right across the Western world, and we have had at least forty years of church growth principles and practice. We can't seem to make disciples based on a consumerist approach to the faith. We plainly cannot consume our way into discipleship. All of us must become more active in the equation of becoming lifelong followers of Jesus. Consumption is detrimental to discipleship.[20]

Hirsch proposed that Christian leaders end the typical approach of seeking to attract people to church by innovation in programing; rather, they should go back to the biblical discipleship model that calls us to go out of our church buildings into the world to make disciples of people. As intimated above, other scholars and Christian leaders are also calling the church back to biblical discipleship.[21] Biblical discipleship includes evangelism and spiritual leadership. While evangelism focuses on leading people to Christ, discipleship involves much more: it entails not only leading people to Christ but also helping them to grow spiritually, equipping them to be responsible for both their own growth and the growth of others, and teaching them to become disciple-makers.

An interesting and positive aspect of the need for discipleship and strong spiritual leadership among Seventh-day Adventist churches comes from the research of Joseph Kidder. Between 2003 and 2007, Kidder and a team of graduate research assistants surveyed churches in the North American Division that had maintained a growth rate from 3 to 5 percent for five consecutive years. Their research revealed that 80 percent of churches in the North American Division are in decline and only 20 percent are thriving. However, they discovered that the thriving churches all had the following four dominant factors: effective and empowering leadership, passionate and authentic spirituality, committed and active laity,

---

20   Hirsch, p. 45.
21   See Jim Putman and Bobby Harrington, *DiscipleShift: Five steps that helps to make disciples who make disciples* (Grand Rapids, MI: Zondervan, 2013); Randy Pope. *Insourcing: Bringing discipleship back to the local church* (Grand Rapids, MI: Zondervan, 2013); Russell Burrill, *Radical disciples for revolutionary churches* (Fallbrook, CA: Hart Research Center, 1996).

and God–exalting worship.[22] Notice that effective and empowering leadership is a core factor among thriving Seventh-day Adventist churches in the North American Division. But also notice that these churches had strong spirituality, active and committed laity, and God-exalting worship—all of which implies strong and stable spiritual leadership. The point that I am making is that effective spiritual leadership is necessary for a healthy and thriving church.

Concerning the issue of worship and music, Kidder's research revealed that a contemporary worship service is not necessary for a thriving church. However, spirituality and good leadership are essential:

> Our research clearly demonstrates that the worship experience is a vital part of growing congregations. But contrary to the perception that such churches are contemporary in their method of worship, we discovered that the style is not essential. What is, however, is the quality of the worship experience, not its placement on the traditional-contemporary continuum. If the heart of the believer touches the heart of God, worship will take place. Though style is not mandatory for growth, excellence, and purpose, prayer, hope, and professionalism are vital.[23]

Pastors should focus on being effective leaders in discipleship and worship in accordance with the principles and methods found in the Bible.

I have emphasized the statements and research of Christian leaders from various denominational backgrounds because the seeker-sensitive approach and the attractional model have beguiled many pastors from all denominations into mistakenly putting their focus on drawing a crowd through improving programming in their worship services and appealing to the wants of people. However, pastors should focus on being effective leaders in discipleship and worship in accordance with the principles and methods found in the Bible. It is time to free ourselves from the pressure of following the latest program or strategy for church growth; and, with this new-found freedom, concentrate on leading out in discipleship, worship, and music in a manner that reflects an understanding of biblical principles and best practices.

---

22   Joseph S. Kidder, *The big four: Secrets to a thriving church family* (Hagerstown, MD: Review and Herald Publishing, 2011).
23   Kidder, p. 14.

CHAPTER 3

An Open Letter to Dr. Jesse Wilson, Chairman of the Pastoral Evangelism Leadership Council, Oakwood University

From Michael G. Coleman, Pastor of the Mount of Olives Seventh-day Adventist Church, Brooklyn, New York, Northeastern Conference

February 19, 2013

Part 1

Dear Dr. Jesse Wilson,

Greetings in the name of the Lord Jesus Christ! I pray that this letter finds you and your family in the best of health and in good spirits.

I am writing an open letter in the form of a treatise to you with the intention that all who read it may join in the conversation and share their opinion on important issues that confront the Seventh-day Adventist Church and the shepherds of its flock. I intend to deal with some controversial issues with humility, sincerity, sensitivity, respect, and good humor.

I hope that this will be a constructive conversation in which all readers of this letter will come away understanding the issues a little better and understanding each other far better than we do. Whether or not we come to an agreement on the issues, I trust that the conversation will add value to our collective relationship.

More than a year ago you and I had a brief conversation in the Oakwood College Church at the 2011 Pastoral Evangelism Leadership Council (PELC) about PELC's strategy for dealing with the controversy surrounding the invitation of Bishop T.D. Jakes to be a speaker and facilitator at the PELC annual meetings. The invitation had been canceled partly in response to some protest concerning it and out of sensitivity to the need for a broader discussion. At that time, you requested of me to send you a synopsis of our conversation and some of the points that I thought might be useful in addressing the issue. I apologize for allowing more than a year to pass without sending you what you had requested. However, I still have an interest in initiating a broad conversation on a range of issues concerning what appears to be a divide in the Adventist Church over worship styles, preaching styles, music, and the church's response to the variety of contemporary phenomena.

My interest was piqued as I listened on Tuesday evening, December 4, 2012 to the closing rhetorical flourishes of a sermon that had hitherto been insightful, inspiring, and moving but had concluded with a mixture of "whooping," fevered gesticulations from both the speaker and several congregants, and heightened rhythmic musical instrumentation, the combination of which, in my thinking, imbibed the spirit of the Charismatic/Glossolalia (speaking in tongues) Movement. Someone might be saying by now, "Coleman, the preacher was just whooping! Don't make a mountain out of a molehill! Whooping is a part of the African American preaching tradition! Leave it alone and let there be peace on earth!" Well, let's look a little deeper!

For the benefit of those who may not be familiar with the term *whooping*, I offer a practical definition. Whooping is rhythmic vocal flourishes that are usually presented towards the conclusion of a sermon; in this phenomenon, preachers, while speaking, sound as if they are about to sing, but they often create a crescendo of ecstatic rhythmic utterances designed to elicit an oral emotional response from their audience.

By representing the closing rhetorical flourishes of the speaker mentioned above as "imbibing" the spirit of the Charismatic/Glossolalia Movement I do not wish to convey that the speaker spoke in charismatic tongues. Rather, I contend that the speaker's concluding rhetorical flourishes were layered with a by-product of the same movement that engendered glossolalia, sensational public healing, exhibitionist exorcism, swooning/slaying in the spirit, and ridiculous contemporary charismatic phenomena such as the uncontrollable laughter of the Toronto Blessing. I am not merely concerned with the speaker's brand of whooping but with the system and philosophy that produced this phenomenon.

In the section below, I will bring clarity to my provocative categorization by differentiating salient stylistic and emotive elements in African American preaching—such as pathos, celebration, narration, and call and response—from the practices of Charismatic/Glossolalia preaching. I will argue below that many of the principles and practices of the charismatic movement are inconsistent with Scripture and are a part of a counterfeit revival whose emergence has been predicted in the Bible, especially in Revelation, and in the writings of Ellen G. White; therefore, the practices of this movement should be rejected.

I will also argue that many of the forms and practices in African American preaching can be gladly employed by Adventist preachers because they are not incongruent with the core values of Adventism and because they can be differentiated from the practices of the Charismatic Movement. However, there are some practices in the black preaching tradition that are inconsistent with the principles of Scripture and impede the advancement of the great gospel commission. I will also highlight the fact that the Charismatic Movement has impacted virtually every Christian denomination; therefore, we need to be careful that our expressions and practices are not layered with or influenced by the spirit and forms of this movement.

My discourse on charismatic worship will transition into a discussion of contemporary worship and music. I will deal with the question of how drums should be used in worship. In other words, the issue is not whether or not to employ drums in worship but rather, how best can they be utilized to glorify God. In similar manner, I will argue that in our quest to modernize our worship services with Contemporary Christian Music, we should be careful to select only music that is congruent with our core values and Biblical principles.

Black Celebratory Preaching and the Issue of Whooping

Anyone who has heard the majestic, pathos-infused, celebratory preaching of Dr. Martin Luther King, Jr., can hardly forget his messages. Who can forget his sermon about the Good Samaritan entitled "On Being a Good Neighbor"? Who can forget his message entitled, "The Drum Major Instinct"? And who can forget his soaring and inspiring words in his "I Have a Dream" speech or in my favorite of his messages—the sublime extemporaneous speech given on the night before the day of his death, in which he concluded in a crescendo of hope in the face of death threats:

> Well, I don't know what will happen now. We've got some difficult days ahead. But it doesn't matter with me now. Because I've been to the mountaintop. And I don't mind. Like anybody, I would like to live a long life. Longevity has its place. But I'm not concerned about that now. I just want to do God's will. And He's allowed me to go up the mountain. And I've looked over. And I've seen the promised land! I may not get there with you. But I want you to know tonight, that we as a people, will get to the Promised Land! And I'm happy, tonight. I'm not worried about anything. I'm not fearing any man. Mine eyes have seen the glory of the coming of the Lord!

Martin King's sermons and speeches epitomize what both Henry H. Mitchell and Mervin A. Warren consider the best in the African American preaching tradition.[24] King's messages address relevant social, political, economic, and spiritual issues from a Biblical perspective and with a blend of pathos and celebration. These messages also called humanity to justice, ethical living, and redemption in Christ, with the rhythm, cadence, and musical tone of the pathos/celebratory tradition in African American preaching.

Yet, as Mervin Warren has observed, King deliberately sought to avoid what he considered to be emotionalism in much of the black preaching and worship of his time. Warren also suggested that he later moderated his views and embraced more emotional expressions in worship and preaching than he initially would have.[25] King sought to strike a balance between emotion and intellectual substance in his preaching. The influence of Benjamin E. Mays and George D. Kelsey, solid African American professors at Morehouse College and also excellent preachers, helped to shape a preaching style in King that was intellectually robust, pathos-infused, and celebratory; yet, one that avoided emotional excess. For example, although King's preaching was rhythmic and musical in tone he did not engage in what is known as whooping. This fact should not be surprising in light of King's clear choice to avoid emotionalism and in light of his mission to proclaim a gospel message that has universal appeal.

Let us for a moment imagine Martin King whooping on his "I Have a Dream" message before the large and variegated audience that listened to him at the Lincoln Memorial in Washington, D.C., in 1963. Whooping would have given his message a parochial, localized, and sensationalized appeal. His profound and moving message would have been tinctured by the flair of emotionalism, and thus the universal appeal that is embedded in this message would have been lost sight of by many.

Seventh-day Adventist ministers are called to preach the "everlasting gospel" of the three angels' messages of Revelation 14 to "every nation, tribe, language and people (NIV)." Nothing should be allowed to diminish the universal appeal of our message. The best preachers in our denomination, both past and present, black and white, have not subscribed to whooping or emotional excess at the times and on the occasions that I have heard them.

---

24 Henry Mitchell has highlighted key attributes of African American preaching. See his references to Martin Luther King, Jr., in *Black Preaching: The Recovery of a Powerful Art* (Nashville: Abington Press, 1990), pp. 82, 108, 130. Mervin Warren has written a biography about King's preaching ministry. See *King Came Preaching* (Downers Grove, Illinois: InterVarsity Press, 2001).
25 Warren, pp. 28, 29, 54.

Let me randomly list some pastors, evangelists, and public speakers that I am thinking of at the moment that have served in America. My list is far from comprehensive, and I do not mean to exclude others: Charles Bradford, C. D. Brooks, Henry Wright, Ron Halverson, Joe Crews, H.M.S. Richards Jr., Walter Pearson, John Nixon, Benjamin Reeves, E. E. Cleveland, Ron Smith, Clifford Jones, Mark Finley, Dwight Nelson, Randy Roberts, Randall Stafford, Sylvia Barnes, Deborah Harris, Randy Skeete, Melvin Hayden, Glen Samuels, Jose Rojas, and Samuel Hutchins.

Nothing should be allowed to diminish the universal appeal of our message.

If my recollection serves me well, the only Adventist preacher in the past that came close to whooping at times was Jerry Lee. Incidentally, one interesting clip on YouTube appears to have a well-known Adventist preacher speaking in charismatic tongues. I have seen the clip, but I cannot determine with certainty that the voice I hear speaking in tongues is the preacher's voice, though other people have said that they have heard the preacher in question speak in tongues on another occasion. However, in recent times an increasing number of our black Adventist preachers are whooping and using Pentecostal/Charismatic flourishes in their preaching as they look for commonality with our non-Adventist colleagues.

Henry Mitchell makes some interesting remarks concerning the chanted or tonal tradition in African American preaching. Mitchell identifies whooping along with moaning as part of a tonal stylistic technique in black preaching. He points out that the most sought-after African American preachers use "intonation only in climatic utterance, or celebration, if they use it at all." Later, in the same paragraph, Mitchell states, "Yet most churches no longer demand tonality, if indeed they ever did. Thus the precise present significance of this feature is very difficult to assess."[26]

Based on a study of a collection of taped sermons of black preachers, Mitchell states "intonation seems seldom to be taken seriously by acknowledged leaders of the Black pulpit" and "this study made readily apparent that many Black congregations no longer require intonation for a religiously celebrative experience."[27] The point Mitchell is making is that whooping is not something that has been in demand or has been taken very seriously among modern African American congregations. Whoop-

---

26 Mitchell, *Black Preaching* (Nashville, TN, Abingdon Press) p. 91.
27 Mitchell, Ibid. p. 91.

ing probably has more of an entertainment value and is certainly not in the league of more enduring qualities of Black preaching such as "call and response"—a characteristic that most African American preachers and students of Black preaching know to be an integral component of black preaching and worship.

Among the characteristics that scholars identify as important qualities of the black pulpit tradition are: call and response, pathos, a narrative habit, a celebratory tone, and messages that show sensitivity to issues of social, economic, and political justice from a Biblical perspective. All of these characteristics seem to me to be congruent with the core values of Adventism. At least none of them is incongruent with Adventism. However, whooping seems to be more on the side of emotionalism and entertainment.

The edition of Mitchell's book that I have quoted from above, *Black Preaching: the Recovery of a Powerful Art*, is a 1990-updated combination of Mitchell's two previous books: *Black Preaching* (1970) and *The Recovery of Preaching* (1977). The thoughts expressed are therefore drawn from Mitchell's analysis of African American preaching from its inception in America to the 1990s. It would be interesting to know what most African American congregations think about whooping today, in the second decade of the twenty-first century. It is interesting that in the 1990s Mitchell observed that a new form of whooping seemed to be on the horizon:

> Since I completed the study of tapes previously mentioned, some twenty-five years ago, an exception has evolved: organ accompaniment to the sermonic celebration. At times this can influence the preacher to move in the direction of rhythmic meter, engaged in spontaneously. All too often it is the brainchild of the musician. And just as often it is hardly to be thought of as a legitimate offspring of the African American pulpit tradition. More appropriate may be the accusation that it is the child of Hollywood and the media.[28]

I agree with the argument that the musical accompaniment brand of whooping has some of the sensational features of "Hollywood and the media" and that it is not a "legitimate offspring of the African American pulpit tradition." As mentioned earlier, I think whooping detracts from the universal appeal of the Advent message and lends itself to emotionalism. Now, when whooping is combined with musical accompaniment, it further sensationalizes or emotionalizes the message and thus compounds

---

28 Mitchell, Ibid, p. 92.

the level of distortion to the universal appeal of the Advent message. In other words, I believe that what might be dubbed "simple whooping" (a moderate use of intonation at the climatic part of the message without musical accompaniment) has been taken to a greater level of excess under the influence of the Pentecostal/Charismatic Movement. Let us, therefore, take a look for a moment at the Pentecostal/Charismatic/Glossolalia Movement and the issue of a counterfeit revival from the perspective of Bible prophecy, Adventist history, and the writings of Ellen G. White. This topic will also lead us into a discussion of contemporary worship styles and music.

Charismatic Worship and Preaching—The Rise of a Counterfeit Revival

Seventh-day Adventists believe that the birth of the Adventist Church, with its mission to prepare the world for the second coming of Christ through the proclamation of present truth, has been predicted in the tenth chapter of Revelation. The Great Disappointment of 1844 is symbolized in the scene of Revelation 10 where John takes the little book from the angel and eats it, and it was sweet in his mouth but made his stomach bitter. Immediately following this, the angel said to John, "Thou must prophesy again before many peoples, and nations, and tongues, and kings" (vs. 11, KJV). This signified that in spite of the Great Disappointment Adventism would become a global movement as it preached the "everlasting gospel" and evangelized the world.

In spite of the misunderstanding of William Miller and many Advent believers concerning what event was to occur in 1844, and in spite of the bitter disappointment that many of these believers experienced when Jesus did not return on October 22, 1844, Ellen White emphatically states in *The Great Controversy,* "Of all the great religious movement since the days of the apostles, none have been more free from human imperfection and the wiles of Satan than was that of the autumn of 1844."[29] This statement is significant in its categorical affirmation of the Great Disappointment and the Advent movement. It is also significant because after the Great Disappointment there were many former Advent believers who left the movement and refused to subscribe to the new understanding of what actually occurred in 1844: namely, the commencement of the antitypical Day of Atonement, which involved both the cleansing of the heavenly sanctuary and the pre-Advent investigative judgment.

---

29   Ellen White, *The Great Controversy* (Nampa, ID, Pacific Press Publishing Assn. 2002), p. 401.

Ellen White had a vision in 1845 that showed that many of the former Advent believers who left the Advent movement after the Great Disappointment actually ended up joining in a false revival movement that had been embraced by many of the denominations of that time. The entire vision is too long to be quoted, so the following quotation is an excerpt of the vision (found in *The Day-Star*, March 14, 1846. Most of this is also in *Early Writings*, p. 54-57):

> And I saw a cloudy chariot with wheels like flaming fire. Angels were all about the chariot as it came where Jesus was; he stepped into it and was borne to the Holiest where the Father sat. Then I beheld Jesus as he was before the Father a great High Priest. On the hem of his garment was a bell and a pomegranate, a bell and a pomegranate. Then Jesus shewed me the difference between faith and feeling. And I saw those who rose up with Jesus send up their faith to Jesus in the Holiest, and praying, Father give us thy spirit. Then Jesus would breathe on them the Holy Ghost. In the breath was light, power and much love, joy and peace. Then I turned to look at the company who were still bowed before the throne. **They did not know that Jesus had left it. Satan appeared to be by the throne trying to carry on the work of God. I saw them look up to the throne and pray, My Father give us thy spirit. Then Satan would breathe on them an unholy influence. In it there was light and much power, but no sweet love, joy and peace. Satan's object was to keep them deceived and to draw back and deceive God's children. I saw one after another leave the company who were praying to Jesus in the Holiest, go and join those before the throne and they at once received the unholy influence of Satan.** (DS March 14, 1846, par. 1, emphasis supplied)

This to me is a most interesting quotation; in it, Ellen White affirms that a counterfeit revival movement had begun shortly after the Great Disappointment in 1844. She showed that Satan deceived many Christians who neglected to heed the atonement/judgment message when it was proclaimed after the Great Disappointment. Ellen White states above that these deceived Christians prayed, "My Father give us thy spirit. Then Satan would breathe on them an unholy influence. In it was light and much power, but no sweet love, joy, and peace."

Ellen White had another vision on March 24, 1849, in which she gave more detail on the characteristics of the counterfeit revival:

I saw that Satan was working through agents in a number of ways. He was at work through ministers who have rejected the truth and are given over to strong delusions to believe a lie that they might be damned. While they were preaching or praying, some would fall prostrate and helpless, not by the power of the Holy Ghost, but by the power of Satan breathed upon these agents, and through them to the people. While preaching, praying, or conversing, some professed Adventists who had rejected present truth used mesmerism to gain adherents, and the people would rejoice in this influence, for they thought it was the Holy Ghost. Some even that used it were so far in the darkness of deception of the devil that they thought it was the power of God, given to them to exercise. They had made God altogether such a one as themselves and had valued His power as a thing of naught. (*Early Writings*, p. 43).

One of the most referenced quotations that Seventh-day Adventists point to when warning about the extremes of the Pentecostal/Charismatic Movement is a statement of Ellen White concerning the characteristics of the worship service at a camp meeting in Indiana in 1900. The kind of worship that occurred at this camp meeting was orchestrated by a group of Seventh-day Adventists who believed in the Holy Flesh Doctrine. The practical implication of this doctrine was that the believer could attain an experience in worship that would take him or her to a state of sinlessness. Let us look at what was going on in the worship service based on a report and vision from Ellen White. Here are some excerpts from Ellen White's commentary on these meetings, found in *Selected Messages*, vol. 2, 35–37:

The manner in which the meetings in Indiana have been carried on, with noise and confusion, does not commend them to thoughtful, intelligent minds. There is nothing in these demonstrations which will convince the world that we have the truth. Mere noise and shouting are no evidence of sanctification, or of the descent of the Holy Spirit. Your wild demonstrations create only disgust in the minds of the unbelievers. The fewer of such demonstrations there are, the better it will be for the actors and for the people in general. ...

The things you have described as taking place in Indiana, the Lord has shown me would take place just before the close of probation. Every uncouth thing will be demonstrated. There will be shouting, with drums, music, and dancing. The senses of rational beings will become so confused that they cannot be trusted to make right decisions. And this is called the moving of the Holy Spirit.

The Holy Spirit never reveals itself in such methods, in such a bedlam of noise. This is an invention of Satan to cover up his ingenious methods for making of none effect the pure, sincere, elevating, ennobling, sanctifying truth for this time. Better never have the worship of God blended with music than to use instruments to do the work which last January was represented to me would be brought into our camp meetings. The truth for this time needs nothing of this kind in its work of converting souls. A bedlam of noise shocks the senses and perverts that which if conducted aright might be a blessing. The powers of satanic agencies blend with the din and noise, to have a carnival, and this is termed the Holy Spirit's working.

Let us notice that Ellen White links the characteristics of the Indiana camp meeting worship services to the false revivals that will take place "just before the close of probation." Then she states, "There will be shouting, with drums, music, and dancing. The senses of rational beings will become so confused that they cannot be trusted to make right decisions. And this is called the moving of the Holy Spirit." Certainly, we can see in the Indiana worship services many of the same things that now exist in contemporary Pentecostal/Charismatic worship services. However, charismatic tongues-speaking or glossolalia is now a prominent hallmark of this movement.

The Charismatic Movement has impacted virtually every Protestant denomination, including the Seventh-day Adventist Church, and also the Roman Catholic Church. Several of the features present in the Indiana camp meeting are now present at the worship services of some Seventh-day Adventist churches and Seventh-day Adventist camp meetings. Adventists do not speak in tongues but the "shouting, with drums, music, and dancing" is present in many of our services today. The musical synchronized whooping of some of our ministers and the frenzied responses of some of our congregants are reminiscent of the kind of mesmerized activities that some Adventist ministers were doing in order to win converts in Ellen White's day.

> *The Charismatic Movement has impacted virtually every Protestant denomination, including the Seventh-day Adventist Church, and also the Roman Catholic Church.*

Seventh-day Adventist preaching and worship should have passion. Adventists can legitimately embrace the pathos, celebration, and call and response that are a part of the African American church experience. However, the whooping, especially with instrumental accompaniment, should be avoided. Furthermore, the worship style of Seventh-day Adventists should not only reflect enthusiasm but also balance, self-control, harmony, majesty, holiness, penitence, and the joy of salvation.

Pentecostal/Charismatic worship is reminiscent of the kind of worship that the prophets of Baal performed on Mount Carmel. They were challenged by Elijah to build an altar, place a sacrifice on it, and call on their god to consume the sacrifice with fire because the prophets of Baal, Elijah, and all the people had agreed that "the God who answers by fire, He is God" (1 Kings 18:24, NKJV). These prophets of Baal cried out from morning till noon and "leaped about the altar which they had made" (vs. 26), but nothing happened; the sacrifice was not consumed. All they did was make noise and work themselves up into an emotional frenzy. After Elijah taunted them concerning their vain worship and the lack of response from their god, their worship activities became even more frenzied and bizarre: "So they cried aloud, and cut themselves, as was their custom, with knives and lances, until the blood gushed out on them" (vs. 28). But notice that when it was Elijah's time to call on his God he only said a simple prayer and God immediately answered by fire (vs. 36–38).

It is very interesting that the imagery of the fire of God coming down to consume Elijah's sacrifice on Mount Carmel is taken up in the apocalyptic prophecy of Revelation 13. But there is a twist to the story: this time it is the lamb-like beast, the joint coalition of church and the state in the United States, that will call fire down from heaven, not to be a sign of the power of the true God, but as a sign of the power of the first beast, the papacy. Notice that in Revelation 13 all that is done by the lamblike beast has one objective—the worship of the first beast:

> Then I saw another beast coming up out of the earth, and he had two horns like a lamb and spoke like a dragon. And he exercises all the authority of the first beast in his presence, and causes the earth and those who dwell in it to worship the first beast, whose deadly wound was healed. **He performs great signs, so that he even makes fire come down from heaven on the earth in the sight of men.** And he deceives those who dwell on the earth by those signs which he was granted to do in the sight of the beast, telling those who dwell on the earth to make an image to the beast who was wounded by the sword and lived. (Rev. 13:11–14, NKJV [emphasis supplied])

The great issue in Revelation 13 is worship. The lamblike beast (the coalition of church and state in America) will seek to turn the world back to the worship of the first beast (the papacy). Two ways in which the first beast will attempt to achieve its objective are through Sunday sacredness and the introduction of spiritualism in worship. Remember that Revelation 16:13–14 states,

> And I saw three unclean spirits like frogs coming out of the mouth of the dragon, out of the mouth of the beast, and out of the mouth of the false prophet. For they are spirits of demons, performing signs, which go out to the kings of the earth and of the whole world, to gather them to the battle of that great day of God Almighty.

Seventh-day Adventists identify the three unclean spirits of Revelation 16 as spiritualism (coming from the dragon), Roman Catholicism/papacy (the beast), and apostate Protestantism (the false prophet). The text explicitly tells us that these unclean spirits are the "spirits of demons, performing signs" to gather the whole world to the battle of God Almighty. Is it any surprise that we find the following phenomena in Charismatic worship: purported miraculous signs, sensational healing, public display of exorcism, swooning, frenzied dancing, glossolalia, music accompanied whooping, and orchestrated trances/ecstatic experiences through heavy rhythmic-playing of loud sounding instruments? Seventh-day Adventist should stay far away from anything that even has the appearance of such worship. We, Seventh-day Adventist ministers, should instruct our flock to worship in a manner that reflects the core beliefs of our faith.

CHAPTER 3

An Open Letter to Dr. Jesse Wilson, Chairman of the Pastoral Evangelism Leadership Council, Oakwood University

From Michael G. Coleman, Pastor of the Mount of Olives Seventh-day Adventist Church, Brooklyn, New York, Northeastern Conference

February 19, 2013

Part 2

Contemporary Music and Worship

Please do not think that I am saying that drums or vibrant emotional expressions should not be a part of our worship service; nor, assume that I am saying that contemporary gospel music should not be a part of our services. Drums, appropriately used, can add a beautiful dimension to our services. Much of contemporary music both secular and religious is heavily rhythmic with the use of drums. But how should drums be used in worship? The sound of today's drums is very conspicuous and almost over-powering in relation to other instruments in the worship service. Should this instrument be used in a way that overpowers other instruments? Or should it be used as a supplement to the less-dominant instruments?

Have you noticed that people who speak in a bass voice tend to speak slowly, and that even when they speed up at times, they always go back to a slow rate of speaking? This phenomenon is virtually universal. Is this a coincidence? No! The bass voice is so powerful that if the speaker spoke fast for a long duration, it would be unpleasant to the ear. People with bass voices tend to speak slowly because both by nature and nurture they have come to hear themselves sounding majestic and they find that they are well-received by their listeners when they speak in a slow manner (Just listen to Barry Black, Henry Wright, Morgan Freeman, or James Earl Jones). Drums have a similar effect as the bass voice. The piano, flute, violin, and harp can be played at a faster rate for a long duration without becoming an irritant to the ear but the drums, the cymbals, and the trumpet, are more conspicuously loud-sounding instruments; they sound better and have a better impact on the ear at a slower rate and at shorter intervals (of course there are exceptions). Furthermore, they often sound better as supplements to other instruments in worship, rather than as the lead instrument.

Much of today's popular music, both secular and religious, has turned the above rationale on its head. The most over-powering instruments are often played at a fast pace for long durations, and while some people have become accustomed to it, we find that in the church today there are many Christians who feel that this constant heavily rhythmic and syncopated musical presentation is both unpleasant and worldly. Balance is needed!

A similar balance is needed in the worship service and in the ministry of music as we find among the members of the human body. Drawing on the apostle Paul's pragmatic analogy in 1 Corinthians 12 between the human body and the members of the body of Christ (the church), we discover that the hands, eyes, ears, mouth, heart, lungs, and feet all have different functions in the human body. The eyes, hands, mouth, and feet definitely have leading roles in the body but how could they survive without the heart and the lungs? Yet, the heart, as indispensable and powerful as it is, was not designed to take the very conspicuous role of the hands or the mouth. Can you imagine what would happen to the body if the beating of the heart were amplified and the power of the heart were made more conspicuous? The impact of the heart would probably be similar to the sound, movement, power, and visual splendor of the Niagara Falls. Which member of the body (besides the brain) could compete with that? The heart would overpower the presence of the mouth, hand, eye, and foot.

Now, the ear is a far more conspicuous member of the body than the heart, but the ear is less prominent than the eye, mouth, foot, and hand. Each member of the human body has its place and function. When they all work together in their proper function and place, there is homeostasis, but when they are out of harmony, there is disease. Likewise, in the normal ebb and flow of worship, the drums, cymbals, and trumpets would do best as complementary instruments. In other words, the softer sounding instruments should take the lead and the loud-sounding instruments should be like the heart in the body.

Many of my colleagues have made the use of drums in the worship service a sort of sign as to whether one is conservative or progressive. They frequently paint a very simplistic and biased picture that those who have concerns about the use of drums in the worship service really don't want drums in the church at all. My colleagues allege that such people are conservative, legalistic, and Eurocentric. These colleagues claim to be progressive, more informed, and more democratic than those who seem to have concerns about the way drums and certain contemporary music are employed in worship.

> *Many of my colleagues have made the use of drums in the worship service a sort of sign as to whether one is conservative or progressive.*

Yet, I am aware of the fact that there are many churches where the drums and certain contemporary music were introduced in worship with little or no discussion and with little or no support from the Bible and the Spirit of Prophecy. In many of these churches, the worship service is horizontally directed toward the pastor and the musicians rather than vertically directed toward God. Expressions such as "let's give the Lord a hand praise," meaning let's clap, is more often directed toward the satisfaction of those leading out than to the praise of God. Often, in these churches, those who subscribe to the contemporary changes that the pastor has launched, seem to curry the pastor's favor and those who disagree with the changes, experience the pastor's displeasure. To be fair, some pastors who want to maintain a traditional worship service, tend to be less than democratic in their leadership style when faced with opposition. However, the point needs to be made that the "progressives" often follow the very behavior and leadership styles of which they accuse traditional/conservative pastors.

Today, many pastors and musicians are attempting to modernize their church's worship service with contemporary music. However, the scenario that one finds in a lot of these churches is that little care is given to whether or not the songs and musical compositions are congruent with Adventist core values. My family and I sing many contemporary worship songs in our worship at home but we are deliberately selective so that we do not bring into our worship that which partakes of the worldly musical genres such as the rhythm & blues, hip-hop, reggae, calypso, disco, rap, jazz, rock, salsa, and much of secular classical music, even if the lyrics are doctrinally correct. By the way, we also intentionally avoid employing in our worship certain classical religious music that is laden with Roman Catholic themes.

My family and I choose to avoid worldly dance music even when it is combined with good lyrics because the Bible says in 1 John 2:15–17:

> Do not love the world or the things in the world. If anyone loves the world, the love of the Father is not in him. For all that is in the world—the lust of the flesh, the lust of the eyes, and the pride of life—is not of the Father but is of the world. And the world is passing away, and the lust of it; but he who does the will of God abides forever. (NKJV)

Those who compose both the instrumentation and the lyrics of worldly music deliberately put a potent package together to promote the lust of the flesh, the lust of the eyes, and the pride of life. But all too often, both the innocent unsuspecting Christian and the nominal Christian listen to a hybrid of worldly instrumentation and religious lyrics without realizing that the former director of the angelic choir, Satan, knows better than to turn Christians off by giving them a total blend of rock or hip-hop or R & B, so he mixes just a modicum of these worldly genres with some religiously beautiful lyrics, and many of us end up drinking this little drop of poison in a very tasty drink.

I realize that some contemporary gospel musical compositions were designed specifically for the praise and worship of God and therefore they have an instrumental and lyrical arrangement that is more conducive to these ends. But there are many other contemporary Christian songs that were designed primarily to sell albums; hence, the objective of these has much more to do with entertaining the listener than praising God. I also realize that for many Christians the instrumental composition is a non-factor as long as the lyrics are religiously coherent.

However, these Christians would do well to consider a fact that is really self-evident: namely, that one powerful feature of the arts is their ability to communicate without words. In other words, an artistic painting needs no words to communicate a message; neither does a sculpture, nor an instrumental composition. This kind of communication by the arts is not perfect or flawless, but it is a fact that music without words can communicate ideas, create moods, stir emotions, elevate or degrade both mind and feelings. Of course, "association" helps music to communicate its message but association is not the cause of the heightened suspense and fright that one feels when a certain kind of music is played in a horror film. The very instrumental composition of that music was designed to create suspense in any audience, regardless of whether or not the audience has ever heard this kind of musical composition before; and, regardless of whether the audience lives in West Africa or the United States.

J. Peter Burkholder states, "The shocking quality of a loud sound, while potentially evoking similar antecedents, is essentially independent of association."[30] Love songs tend to carry a certain instrumental arrangement that conveys to the listener that the song is romantic, independent of whether or not he or she has ever heard a similar musical composition

---

30   J. Peter Burkholder, "A Simple Model for Associative Musical Meaning," in *Approaches to Meaning in Music*, Edited by Byron Almén & Edward Pearsall (Bloomington and Indianapolis: Indiana University Press, 2006) p. 77.

before or whether he or she speaks Mandarin or English. It therefore should not be a surprise to us that certain instrumental composition can convey to the listener feelings of holiness, majesty, peace, purity, love, and self-control—or conversely—perversion, covetousness, fear, hatred, destructiveness, rebellion against authority, cynicism, excess, deviancy, lust, frivolity, pride, and irreverence.

I recently heard one of our denomination's leaders make an interesting point regarding "association" and the challenge of those who come into the church from the world. He stated that frequently those who come to the faith from the world have "a problem of association." For example, if they were accustomed to going to clubs and listening to R&B, when they come into the church they try to get as far as possible from whatever reminds them of this experience. However, the Adventist who was born and bred in the church tends to have little problem with the R&B or similar music. I believe this is a valid point, but I think it is incomplete.

First of all, while converts from the world are often trying to get as far as possible from any resemblance of their previous experience, these very ones know by experience the pitfalls and temptations in the world that can ensnare the unsuspecting Adventist who tends to crave exposure to the unfamiliar. Thus, while a new convert might have "a problem with association," many Adventists who were born and bred in the church tend to have a problem in craving exposure for the unfamiliar, such a craving often leads them away from Christ or leads them to bring the world into the church. Perhaps the most important point on this particular issue is that both groups—the Adventists who came out of the world and the ones who were bred in the church—need each other. The church, the body of Christ, is made stronger by both groups, especially when both groups come together and share the richness of their experience.

Many African American Adventists today believe that the heavily syncopated rhythmic music that is found in popular secular songs and is also present in numerous Contemporary Christian songs, is a legitimate component of the spiritual heritage of Blacks. However, let us get a historical perspective on this issue from an African-American musicologist and former professor and choir director at Oakwood University, Eurydice Osterman:

> The prevailing assumption that rock music is a legitimate expression of African-American heritage ignores the significant differences that exist between the two. African-American heritage music is predominantly melodic and is based upon the rhythm of the dia-

lect. Rock music, on the other hand, is based upon and is driven by a beat that overshadows and dominates all other musical elements.

The roots of the rock beat are to be found not in the religious music of the African-American heritage, but in secular and often irreligious music known as "Rhythm and Blues." This music became the expression of those Blacks who strayed from or rejected the Christian faith. They wanted to become respected entertainers by playing secular music. The mood of the Blues is one of sadness, punctuated by a regular, heavy beat. The emphasis is on the pleasures of the world, especially of illicit sex before or outside marriage.

After World War II, White entertainers, fascinated by the beat of the Blues, began to copy this style of music and augmented the instrumentation with electric guitars, bass, and drums. Soon this music was popularized by singers like Bill Haley, Chuck Berry, Buddy Holly, and, especially Elvis Presley. From this fusion, a new musical style was born—Rock and Roll. The latter differs from the Blues because of its constant drum beat that makes it conducive to dancing.

The distinction that we find in African-American music between the religious Negro Spiritual and the secular, irreligious Rock and Roll reminds us of the simple fact that in all cultures we can expect to find some music which is pro-Christian and some which is anti-Christian in its values. This is the result of the fall of humankind which is present in every age, country, and culture. "All have sinned and fall short of the glory of God" (Rom 3:23).[31]

> *In our African American culture, we have, on one hand, the pathos-infused Negro spirituals, some traditional gospel music, and some Contemporary Christian Music, that uphold our core values.*

Eurydice Osterman's point is clear: in almost every culture one can find music that is complementary with the core values of Christianity and

---

31   Eurydice Osterman (African American Adventist Musicologist, former Professor of Music at Oakwood College, former director of the Oakwood College Choir & the Aeolians), in *The Christian & Rock Music* (Berrien Springs, MI, Biblical Perspectives, 2000), p. 302.

conversely, music that opposes such values. In our African American culture, we have, on one hand, the pathos-infused Negro spirituals, some traditional gospel music, and some Contemporary Christian Music, that uphold our core values, but, on the other hand, we also have the secular R&B, hip-hop, jazz, and related hybrids that do not reflect the principles of our belief system. When the above secular genres or related hybrids of them are blended with some components of sacred music and Christian lyrics, the music that is produced is often as deleterious to our spirituality as a drop of poison in a glass of all-natural carrot juice is to our health.

Some contemporary worship songs have elements in them that could be modified and made conducive to the core values of Adventists. For example, a pianist, organist, or drum player might adjust the pitch, the cadence, duration, volume, or tempo. They might also add or subtract a particular element in the musical composition. They might purchase drums sets that include hand-drums or they might give study to how different types of drumheads and levels of tension on them produce different volume levels. Church musicians might also pay careful attention to the space that they are working with in the sanctuary. The use of a loud sounding instrument in a small sanctuary in the same way that it is used in a large sanctuary is not prudent because the volume of that instrument will be greater in a smaller space. Furthermore, when the sound of a loud sounding instrument is emanating from one direction at a constant rate for a long duration, those closer to the sound are often disturbed by it while those farther away from it have no problem with it.

The devil often uses issues that require minor modification to create a large-scale disturbance. For example, in the summer of 1997, I conducted an evangelistic tent meeting in Uniondale, New York, that resulted in the baptism of fifty-one precious souls and the planting of a new church. However, the evangelistic meeting had the effect of disturbing the peace of the neighborhood because I kept asking the audio technicians to turn up the volume on the microphone. I did this because I could not hear myself well while preaching. The problem was that the main audio speakers were turned outward from the tent into the neighborhood for most of the time, and if we had monitors (I don't recall) they were not positioned close enough for me to hear myself adequately.

Church musicians, audio technicians, and pastors should give careful attention to matters involving the distribution of sound and decibel levels. However, what frequently happens in many of our churches is that we embrace popular contemporary Christian music that is heavily rhythmic and dominated by loud-sounding instruments without making any modification; and, while these kinds of musical compositions may be okay at a skating rink or at an aerobics class, they can be very disturbing when presented in worship in the sanctuary.

As I move toward a conclusion, let me leave a quotation from Güenter Preuss, an Adventist musicologist, that I think provides a succinct definition of sacred music:

> Sacred music reflects the majesty, harmony, purity, and holiness of God in its melody, harmony, rhythm, text, and performance practices. Its goal is not to entertain or draw attention to the performer's ability, but to glorify God and to inspire believers to conform to the image of God.[32]

---

32   Güenter Preuss (Adventist Musicologist), in *The Christian & Rock Music: A study on Biblical Principles of Music*, ed., Samuel Bacchiocchi (Berrien Springs, MI, Biblical Perspectives, 2000), p. 304.

Conclusion

In the pages above, I have spent a great deal of time discoursing on preaching, music, and worship, with sensitivity to the Adventist African American worship context. Like an automobile driver who is focused on the road in front of him, I might have missed addressing certain issues that did not appear in my blind spot, but I hope that I have addressed the most important issues in a manner that will evoke reflection and elicit constructive debate. Please forgive me if my inclination toward a particular matter might have caused me not to adequately address the other side of the coin. I am particularly concerned about the issues that I have written about because they have both an acute and a chronic impact on the Seventh-day Adventist Church.

First, let's look at the acute impact: as a pastor in New York City at a time when the Seventh-day Adventist Church is about to launch a massive evangelistic thrust in this city in 2013—a thrust which is to be a "symbol" of how we will evangelize urban centers around the world—I am concerned that charismatic worship styles and a concoction of heavily rhythmic loud sounding music will be part of the package that many of our churches present in their public evangelistic meetings. I believe that this would be a grave mistake. We have better, nobler, and more enduring things to offer those who come to our meetings. If we use the aforementioned methods to entertain and attract large crowds, and if they become baptized members of our churches, that which we employed to attract them we will be obliged to maintain to keep them. Consequently, our acute problem will become a chronic problem, which in turn, will inevitably produce more acute problems.

Now, let us look at the chronic impact: The Pastoral Evangelism Leadership Council (formerly known as the Evangelism Council) has been a much-beloved staple for equipping and enlightening a largely Black—and now increasingly multi-ethnic—Adventist ministerial constituency for more than forty years. However, within the last few years, it has come to a crossroads and has opted for a worship style and a preaching agenda that seem to highlight Pentecostal/Charismatic methods.

I have been tremendously enriched from the education and spiritual development I received at Oakwood College (now Oakwood University) as a student in the 1980s, and I have also benefited from much of what I have received over the years at the PELC meetings. I agree with the saying that "Oakwood is the mecca of Black Adventism" and I realize that what transpires at the Pastoral Evangelism Leadership Council impacts a large group that includes Adventist ministers beyond North America, the students at Oakwood University, and alumni dispersed around the world. The apparent move toward a charismatic agenda will inevitably entangle the PELC in matters over which it will have little control. The music-synchronized whooping and charismatic rhetorical flourishes will continue. Frenzied responses to this kind of preaching in the form of 'ecstatic dances" and running in the aisles will become common. And, do not be surprised if one day an Adventist preacher breaks forth in charismatic tongues.

It is, I believe, the very direction that PELC seems to be going in that made the 2011 invitation of T.D. Jakes a matter of great controversy. The Evangelism Council and PELC have had a tradition of inviting non-Adventist speakers to speak at our sessions, and most of my colleagues and I have not had a problem with this policy. However, in a time when PELC seems to be moving in the direction of highlighting charismatic methods, T.D. Jakes represents one of the principal spokespersons of the Charismatic movement—a movement which many Adventists believe to be a counterfeit revival. There are impressionable Adventist pastors in our conferences that already seem too infatuated with the Pentecostal/Charismatic methodology. Now is not the time to tickle their fancies or to dangle temptation before their eyes.

I heard the memorable sermon of Pastor C.D. Brooks entitled "I Want My Church Back" and I remember that he stated the following:

> Harold Lee was addressing this condition not long ago when he said, "Neo-Pentecostalism will be the death of Black Adventism." I wrote that down. We Black people are especially vulnerable because we are such an emotional people. We have been here too long. Divided and separated by racism, by advantage, education, money, and privilege, we have been forced into being reactive, but we have come too close to heaven. Don't let us be cheated now and miss heaven after all we've gone through.

"Neo-Pentecostalism will be the death of Black Adventism."

"Neo-Pentecostalism will be the death of Black Adventism." These are prescient words from a veteran African American Adventist pastor, former union president, and director of the Bradford-Cleveland-Brooks Institute at Oakwood University, Elder Harold Lee. As these words reverberate in my mind, a scene from the film "Apollo 13" (a dramatization of the real story of the 1970 space mission to the moon) comes to view: a critical problem has arisen in the rocket while out in space, thousands of miles from Mission Control in Houston, Texas. The mission to the moon is in jeopardy and the lives of the astronauts on board are at risk. Over the intercom at Mission Control comes the most memorable words from out in space: "HOUSTON! WE HAVE A PROBLEM!" Today as I write this letter, I realize that the mission of our world church is in jeopardy and the ministry of our pastors and evangelists are at risk, so my prayer cries out from New York to Mission Control, not at the PELC at Oakwood University, nor at the General Conference headquarters in Silver Spring, Maryland, but to Mission Control in Heaven: "HEAVEN! WE'VE GOT A PROBLEM!"

May God be merciful to us as we seek through constructive discussion, Bible Conferences, and much prayer to deal with our problem! Thank you for your patience in reading this letter. May the grace of God continue to sustain you, your family, and those who collaborate with you in the planning of the PELC.

Sincerely,

Michael G. Coleman

Summary

In this book, we have reflected on music and worship from different angles. The powerful impact that Contemporary Christian Music has on many churches and individual Christians has inspired me to give careful attention to the question of its appropriateness for both worship and personal use. In light of the strong influence of rock, R&B, and other popular dance genres on CCM, I have emphasized the need to be very selective in our choice of CCM. Specifically, we should make sure that the instrumental composition that carries and accentuates the lyrics is not one that creates a sensual or prideful mood. This is in harmony with 1 John 2:15–16, which admonishes against loving the world, "For all that is in the world—the lust of the flesh, the lust of the eyes, and the pride of life—is not of the Father but of the world."

The need for strong spiritual leadership in worship and music in the church today has motivated me to show from Biblical examples and research that effective spiritual leaders play an important role in equipping the church for worship, music, and discipleship. Therefore, an awesome responsibility rest upon pastors and elders to lead worship and music in their local churches with an understanding of biblical principles and with knowledge of the issues involved.

Finally, the growing influence of the Charismatic/Pentecostal Movement on the way some Adventist pastors and churches are now worshiping has created the necessity to show from the Bible and the writings of Ellen White that the Charismatic/Glossolalia Movement is part of a counterfeit revival and that these influences undermine the pure effect of the gospel. When there is whooping accompanied by rhythmic organ rifts; when there is pronounced and sustained heavily-rhythmic use of drums and bass instruments; and when an atmosphere of emotionalism is created, there will likely be much excitement but little repentance from sin.

Bibliography

Bacchiocchi, Samuel, ed. *The Christian & Rock Music*. Berrien Springs, MI: Biblical Perspectives, 2000.

Bayles, Martha. *Hole in Our Soul: the Loss of Beauty and Meaning in American Popular Music*. New York, Toronto, Oxford: The Free Press, 1994.

Bloom, Allan. *The Closing Of The American Mind*. New York, New York: Simon and Schuster, 1987.

Brown, Callum. *The Death of Christian Britain: Understanding Secularization, 1800–2000*. London and New York: Routledge, 2001.

Burkholder, J. Peter. "A Simple Model for Associative Musical Meaning." Almén, Byron & Pearsall, Edward, ed. *Approaches to Meaning in Music*. Bloomington and Indianapolis: Indiana University Press, 2006.

Burney, Bob. "A Shocking 'Confession' from Willow Greek Community Church," *Town Hall*, October 30, 2007. Retrieved from http://1ref.us/ra, accessed December 19, 2018.

Burrill, Russell. *Radical Disciples for Revolutionary Churches.* Fallbrook, CA: Hart Research Center, 1996.

Cleave, Maureen. "How Does a Beatle Live? John Lennon Lives Like this." *Evening Standard,* March 4, 1966.

Diamond, John. *Behavioral Kinesiology.* New York, New York: Harper & Row, 1979.

Doukhan, Lilianne. *In Tune with God.* Hagerstown, MD: Review and Herald Publishing Association, 2010.

Geiger, Eric, Kelly, Michael, and Nation, Philip. *Transformational Discipleship: How People Really Grow.* Nashville, TN: B&H Books, 2012.

Hawkins, Gary L., Parkinson, Cally. *Reveal: Where are You?* Chicago, Il: Willow Creek Association, 2007.

Hirsch, Alan. *The Forgotten Ways.* Grand Rapids, MI: Brazos Press, 2006.

Randy Pope. *Insourcing: Bringing Discipleship Back to the Local Church* Grand Rapids, MI: Zondervan, 2013.

Kidder, Joseph S. *The Big Four: Secrets to a Thriving Church Family.* Hagerstown, MD: Review and Herald Publishing Association, 2011.

Lucarini, Dan. *Why I Left the Contemporary Christian Music Movement.* New York, New York: Evangelical Press, 2002.

Mitchell, Henry. *Black Preaching: the Recovery of a Powerful Art.* Nashville: Abington Press, 1990.

Nichol, Francis D., ed. *Seventh-day Adventist Bible Commentary*, vol. 7. Washington, D.C.: Review and Herald Publishing Association, 1980), p. 767–8.

Osterman, Eurydice. Bacchiocchi, Samuel, ed. *The Christian & Rock Music.* Berrien Springs, MI: Biblical Perspectives, 2000.

Pielke, Robert. *You Say You Want a Revolution.* Chicago: Nelson-Hall Publishers, 1986.

Pope, Randy. *Insourcing: Bringing Discipleship Back to the Local Church.* Grand Rapids, MI: Zondervan, 2013.

Preuss, Güenter. Bacchiocchi, Samuel, ed. *The Christian & Rock Music: A Study on Biblical Principles of Music*. Berrien Springs, MI, Biblical Perspectives, 2000.

Putman, Jim, Harrington, Bobby. *DiscipleShift: Five Steps That Helps to Make Disciples Who Make Disciples*. Grand Rapids, MI: Zondervan, 2013.

Schwartz, Christian. *Natural Church Development: A Guide to Eight Essential Qualities of Healthy Churches*. Carol Stream, IL: ChurchSmart Resources, 1996.

Stowe, David. *No Sympathy for the Devil*. Chapel Hill, NC: University of North Carolina Press, 2011.

Warren, Rick. *The Purpose Driven Church*. Grand Rapids, MI: Zondervan, 1995.

Warren, Mervin. *King Came Preaching*. Downers Grove, Illinois: InterVarsity Press, 2001.

White, Ellen G. *Acts of the Apostles*. Nampa, ID, Pacific Press Publishing Association.

White, Ellen G. *The Great Controversy*. Nampa, ID, Pacific Press Publishing Association, 2002).

Willard, Dallas. *The Great Omission: Reclaiming Jesus's Essential Teachings on Discipleship*. San Francisco, CA: HarperOne, 2006.

TEACH Services, Inc.
P U B L I S H I N G

We invite you to view the complete
selection of titles we publish at:
www.TEACHServices.com

We encourage you to write us
with your thoughts about this,
or any other book we publish at:
info@TEACHServices.com

TEACH Services' titles may be purchased in
bulk quantities for educational, fund-raising,
business, or promotional use.
bulksales@TEACHServices.com

Finally, if you are interested in seeing
your own book in print, please contact us at:
publishing@TEACHServices.com
We are happy to review your manuscript at no charge.

www.ingramcontent.com/pod-product-compliance
Lightning Source LLC
Chambersburg PA
CBHW042136160426
43200CB00019B/2956